Loud and Quiet

By Jack Challoner

Contents

RSVP
RAINTREE
STECK-VAUGHN
PUBLISHERS
The Steck-Vaughn Company

Austin, Texas

Published by Raintree Steck-Vaughn Publishers, an imprint of Steck-Vaughn Company

Editors: Kim Merlino, Kathy DeVico
Project Manager: Lyda Guz
Electronic Production: Scott Melcer

Photo Credits: cover: top Claire Paxton;
NHPA: bottom Steven Dalton;
J. Allan Cash: pp. 6, 18, 26;
Eye Ubiquitous: p. 5 A. Carroll; p. 19 L. Fordyce; p. 20 Benn Spencer;
p. 24 Jim Merryweather;
Sally and Richard Greenhill: p. 4;
Robert Harding Picture Library: pp. 21, 25 Ron Oulds;
Redferns: p. 22 Leon Morris;
Science Photo Library: p. 12 Richard Megna/Fundamental;
p. 17 Chris Priest;
Tony Stone Images: p. 13 Tim Flach;
Zefa: p. 15 R. Smith; pp. 23, 27, 29 L. Lenz.

Library of Congress Cataloging-in-Publication Data

Challoner, Jack.
Loud and quiet / by Jack Challoner.
p.   cm. — (Start-up science)
Includes index.
ISBN 0-8172-4318-6
1. Sound — Juvenile literature. [1. Sound.   2. Sound — Experiments.
3. Experiments.]   I. Title.   II. Series: Challoner, Jack. Start-up science.
QC225.5.C47   1997
534 — dc20
95-48339
CIP
AC

Printed in Spain
Bound in the United States
1 2 3 4 5 6 7 8 9 0 LB 99 98 97 96

Loud and Quiet

This book will answer lots of questions that you may have about loud and quiet things. But it will also make you think for yourself.

Each time you turn a page, you will find an activity that you can do yourself at home or at school. You may need help from an adult.

When there are lots of loud sounds around you, it is noisy. What makes some sounds louder than others?

Loud Sounds

The more noise something makes, the louder it is. You can hear loud sounds from a long way away. Noisy things sound louder the closer that you are to them.

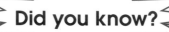

Noisy fireworks

The whizzes and bangs of a fireworks display can be heard from far away. The fireworks make lots of noise as they explode high up in the air.

Takeoff

Airplanes can be very noisy when they take off. The closer you are to them, the louder they sound.

Now try this

You can hear a loud sound when you tap a spoon against a table.

You will need:

a metal spoon, some string

1. Tie a piece of string to the handle of the spoon.

2. Wrap one end of the string around a finger, and press that finger against one ear.

3. Now dangle the spoon from the string. Tap it against the side of a table. What do you hear?

Quiet Things

Things that do not make much noise are quiet. We need to be very close to quiet things and to listen carefully in order to hear them properly.

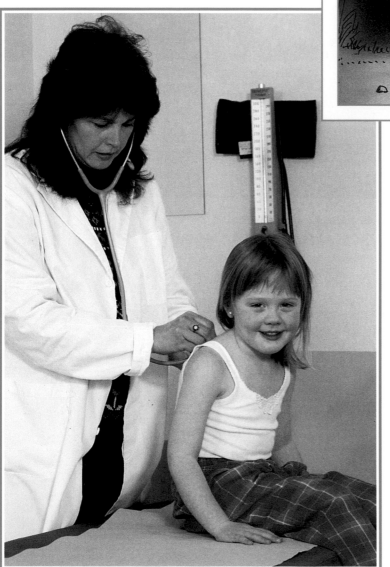

Beating heart

Can you hear your heart beating? This doctor is using an instrument called a **stethoscope.** It makes the girl's quiet heartbeat sound much louder.

Listening quietly

Sometimes you need to be quiet. When someone reads a story out loud, you will not be able to hear unless you listen quietly.

Now try this

You can see for yourself how a stethoscope can help you to hear quiet sounds.

You will need:
a cardboard tube, a watch that ticks

1. Hold one end of the tube gently against your ear.

2. Now put the other end of the tube over the watch. What do you hear?

Making Sound

The more sound something makes, the louder it is. Objects must move backward and forward very quickly, or **vibrate**, to make sound.

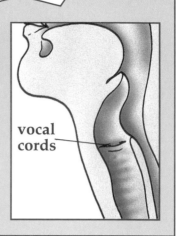

Noisy balloon

A balloon can make a funny sound when you stretch its neck. The rubber at the neck of the balloon vibrates as air escapes from the balloon.

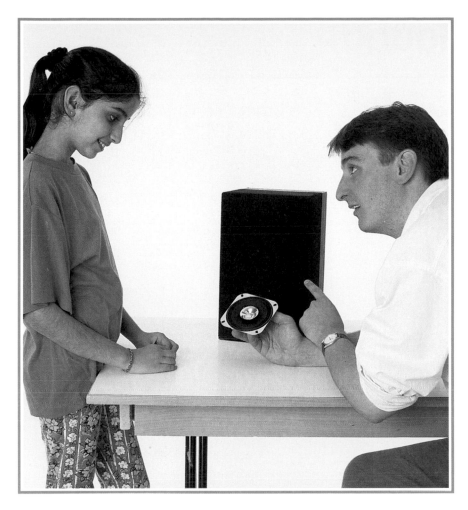

Paper cone

This **loudspeaker** makes sound when the **hi-fi** is switched on. Inside the loudspeaker, there is a paper cone that vibrates to make the sound.

Now try this

You can feel the vibrations of a loudspeaker by using a balloon.

You will need:

a balloon, a hi-fi or portable cassette player

1. Blow up the balloon. Ask an adult to tie the neck of the balloon.

2. Ask an adult to turn on the hi-fi very low. Hold the balloon between one loudspeaker and your ear.

3. Ask an adult to make the hi-fi a little louder. Does the balloon vibrate more or less?

Traveling Sound

An object that vibrates makes sound. The sound travels through the air from the object so that we can hear it. Sounds can also travel through solid objects.

Blowing a whistle

Can you see the man blowing his whistle? The sound the whistle makes travels through the air in all directions, so that the children can hear it.

Did you know?

The fastest cars in the world have rockets to push them along at high speeds. But even the fastest cars cannot travel as fast as sound.

Traveling through wood

This girl is making the table vibrate by tapping it with a pencil. The vibrations travel through the table, and the boy can hear the sound.

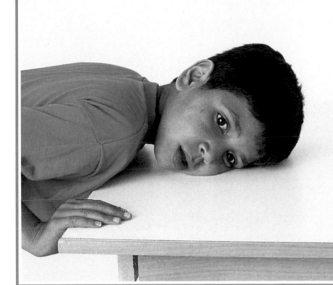

Now try this

Sound travels through the air quite quickly. But sometimes you can see something happen before you can hear the sound.

1. With an adult and a friend, go to a park or your school grounds.

2. Ask your friend to walk about 300 feet (90 m) away from you and to clap. Do you see the hands clap, or do you hear the sound first?

Sound Waves

Any object that vibrates disturbs the air that is around it. The vibrations travel in all directions as invisible **sound waves**. This is how sounds reach us.

Seeing sound waves

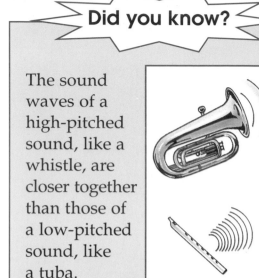

The sound waves of a high-pitched sound, like a whistle, are closer together than those of a low-pitched sound, like a tuba.

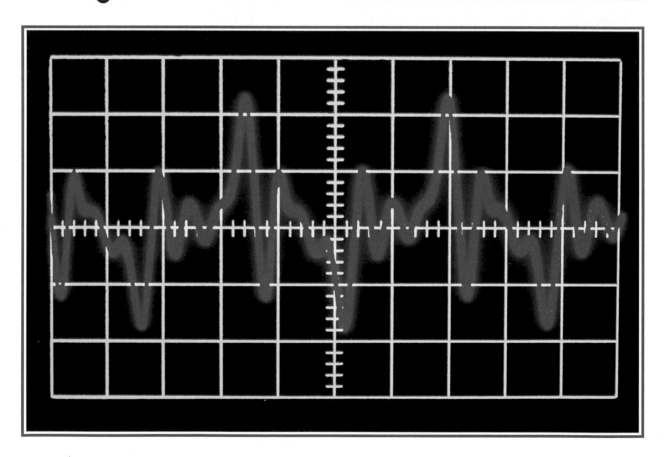

This picture shows sound waves that were made by someone speaking. A machine called an **oscilloscope** shows the sound waves as a line on a screen.

Water waves

When you drop something into water, it disturbs the water and makes waves. The waves travel outward in all directions, just like sound waves.

Now try this

You can see for yourself how water waves are made.

You will need:
a bowl filled with water

1. Roll up your sleeves, and hold one finger just above the water.

2. Touch the surface of the water, and move your finger gently up and down. You should see waves moving outward from your finger.

Bouncing Sound

Sometimes a sound that is traveling through the air will bounce off a hard object, such as a wall. A sound that has bounced off something is called an **echo**.

Some ships bounce sound off the bottom of the ocean, so that they can tell how deep the water is. If the echo returns very soon, it means the water is shallow.

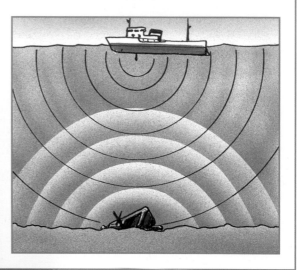

Hearing echoes

This woman is calling to her friend, who has walked into a tunnel. The sound of her voice bounces off the hard stone and comes back as an echo.

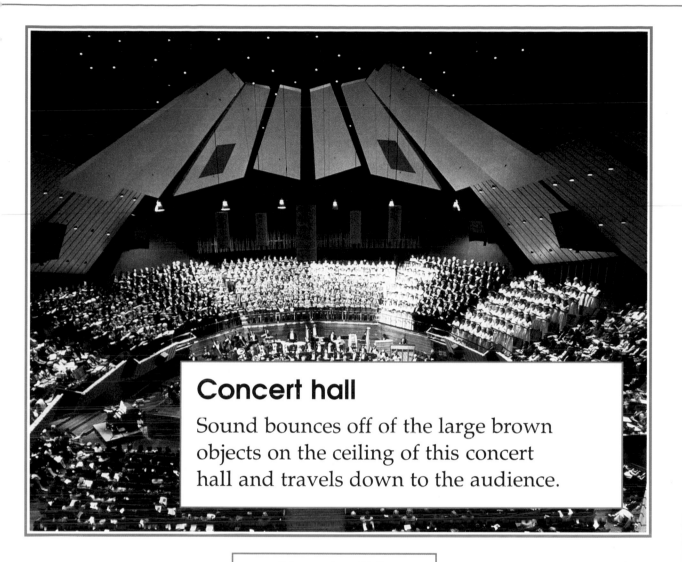

Concert hall

Sound bounces off of the large brown objects on the ceiling of this concert hall and travels down to the audience.

Now try this

Sound only bounces off hard objects, such as walls. It will not bounce off soft objects, such as curtains.

1. Stand in a bathroom, or a large hallway, and clap your hands. Listen carefully for an echo.

2. Try clapping your hands in rooms that have curtains, chairs, or beds. Do you still hear an echo?

How We Hear

We hear sounds with our ears and our brains. Most people can hear loud sounds and quiet sounds. But how do our ears work?

Eardrum

Inside our ears, there is a piece of skin called the **eardrum**. As sound hits it, it vibrates. This sends messages to our brain, so we hear the sound.

Hearing aid

This is a hearing aid. A very small **microphone** inside it picks up sounds, and the hearing aid makes them louder. This helps the man to hear sounds better.

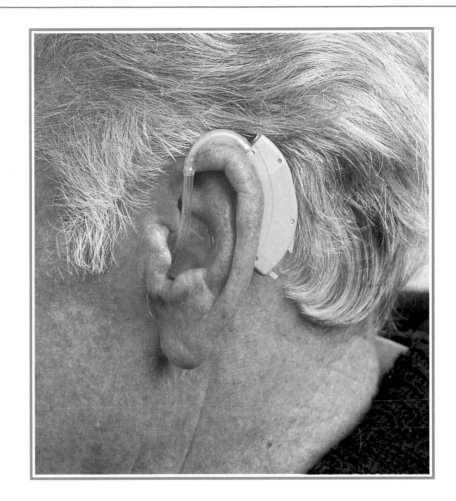

Now try this

You can see how eardrums vibrate as sound hits them.

You will need:
a bowl, plastic food wrap, uncooked rice grains, a hi-fi or portable cassette player

1. Ask an adult to stretch the plastic food wrap over the bowl.

2. Place a few rice grains on top of the bowl. Put it next to the loudspeaker of the hi-fi.

3. Turn the music on so that it is quite loud. What happens to the rice grains?

Animal Ears

There are almost as many types of animal ears as there are different types of animals. Many animals' ears are shaped so that they can catch lots of sound easily.

Did you know?

A crocodile's ears are located just behind its eyes. The ears have flaps of skin that can close to keep the water out.

Big ears

This hare has very large ears. It can hear very well because more sound travels into its large ears than it would into smaller ears.

No ears?

This insect is a cricket. It has no ears on its head. It hears sound with tiny ears on its legs.

Now try this

A hare's large ears mean that it can hear very well. You can see for yourself how this works.

You will need:
a radio

1. Turn on the radio so that the sound is very soft.

2. Sit near the radio so that you can just hear it.

3. Cup one hand behind your ear. How does the radio sound now?

High and Low Sounds

If an object vibrates very quickly, it will make a high-pitched sound. If it vibrates slowly, it will make a low-pitched sound.

Big drum

As the drummer hits the skin of this big drum, the skin vibrates quite slowly. This makes a very low-pitched sound. A bigger drum might make a sound that is too low in pitch for you to hear.

High notes

This opera singer can sing notes that are very high. When we sing high notes, our vocal cords stretch so that they can vibrate more quickly.

Now try this

When you sing a high note, your vocal cords stretch. You can feel this change in your throat.

1. Hold your throat gently between a finger and thumb.

2. Sing a low note. Can you feel your throat vibrating?

3. Now sing a high note. Can you feel your throat change shape?

Music from Strings

Some musical instruments make sounds using strings. Strings held tightly at each end vibrate when they are either plucked with a finger or rubbed with a bow.

Long and short

This harp player makes sounds by plucking the harp strings with her fingers. The short strings make high notes, and the longer strings make lower notes.

Did you know?

A piano has many strings inside it. When a key is pressed, a hammer strikes a string inside and plays a note.

Using a bow

The strings of this violin vibrate as the man moves the bow across them. The man changes each note he plays by pressing his fingers down on different strings.

Now try this

You can see for yourself how shorter strings make higher notes.

You will need:

a shoebox, a rubber band, a pencil

1. Stretch the rubber band over the box, and push the pencil under the rubber band.

2. Now pluck the rubber band. Move the pencil so that you pluck a shorter piece of the rubber band.

Is the note higher or lower than before?

Music from Air

Air in a pipe can be made to vibrate. When it does, it makes a sound. The sound is higher in pitch in a short pipe than it is in a long one.

Covering all of the holes on a recorder with your fingers makes a low note. This is because covering all the holes makes the recorder into a long pipe.

Air in pipes

These organ pipes can make loud sounds as air vibrates inside them. The long pipes make low sounds, and the short pipes make higher sounds.

Mouth music

These trombone players blow through their lips to make the air inside their trombones vibrate. Making the tube longer or shorter changes the notes.

Now try this

You can make your own musical sound from air. Different amounts of air in the bottle make different notes.

You will need:
a clean plastic bottle, water

1. Put some water into the bottle.

2. Put your bottom lip against the neck of the bottle, and blow gently. You should hear a sound.

3. Add more water. Does the sound become higher or lower?

Animal Noises

Most animals make some sort of sound. Usually the sound sends a message to other animals. This is called **communication**.

Noisy snake

Dried skin in this rattlesnake's tail makes a rattling sound as the tail moves. The sound frightens away any animals that might want to attack the snake.

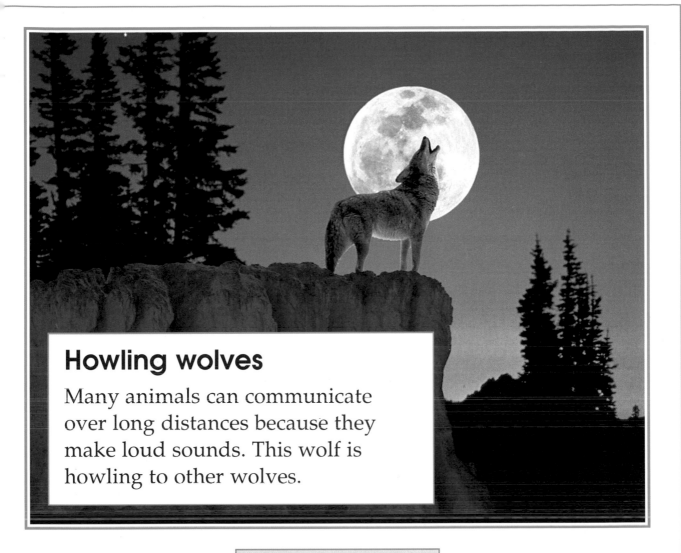

Howling wolves

Many animals can communicate over long distances because they make loud sounds. This wolf is howling to other wolves.

Now try this

You can see for yourself how rattlesnakes make a rattling sound.

You will need:

uncooked rice grains or dried beans, an empty one-liter plastic bottle

1. Put a handful of rice or beans in the bottle.

2. Screw on the lid of the bottle.

3. Shake the bottle, and you will hear a rattling sound. How does it sound when you shake it harder?

Loud and Quiet Places

In places where there is a lot happening, such as a factory, it is noisy. Some places are so noisy that you could hurt your ears if you stayed there for too long.

Protecting our ears

People who work with noisy machines often have to wear **ear protectors**. These keep much of the sound from entering their ears.

Quiet room

This recording studio is a very quiet place. The walls of the studio are very thick, and the door is shut tightly. No outside sounds come in.

Now try this

You can see for yourself how ear protectors work.

You will need:
two polystyrene cups, a clean pair of socks, a radio

1. Push one sock into each cup.

2. Turn on the radio.

3. Hold one cup firmly over each of your ears. Can you still hear the radio clearly?

Recorded Sound

When you play a compact disc or a cassette, you may hear sounds that were made a long time ago. These sounds were recorded by using microphones.

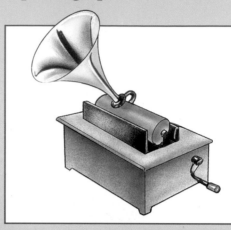
Not too loud

Our ears are very sensitive. Too much loud sound can harm them. So if you use a portable cassette player, you should not play it too loudly.

Using a microphone

Inside this microphone, there is a part called a **diaphragm**, which works like an eardrum. As sound hits the diaphragm, it vibrates. Microphones can be used to record sound.

Now try this

Can you tell what something is just by the sound it makes? Record some different sounds, and see if your friends can guess what they are.

You will need:

a cassette recorder with a microphone, a blank cassette, some objects that will make different noises

1. Ask an adult to help you to set up the cassette recorder, and to record some sounds.

2. Play back the sounds to your friends, and see if they can guess what made each one.

Glossary

communicate To talk or send messages

diaphragm A vibrating disc inside of a telephone, microphone, or loudspeaker

eardrum A delicate skin stretched across the inside of the ear

ear protectors Special pads worn over the ears to protect them from very loud noises

echo A sound that has bounced off a hard surface

erupting Exploding

hi-fi A machine used to listen to radio, cassettes, records, or compact discs

loudspeaker An object that uses electricity to make sounds

microphone A device that changes sound into electricity

oscilloscope A machine that allows sound waves to be shown on a screen

phonograph An early type of record player

sound waves The way in which sound travels through the air

stethoscope An instrument used to listen to the heart or lungs

vibrate To move back and forth very rapidly

vocal cords The part of the human body that produces the voice

Index